GOD IS SPEAKING,
ARE YOU LISTENING?

GOD IS SPEAKING, ARE YOU LISTENING?

A Collection of Testimonies

TRESSA RENEE FERNANDEZ

XULON PRESS

Xulon Press
2301 Lucien Way #415
Maitland, FL 32751
407.339.4217
www.xulonpress.com

Unless otherwise indicated, Scripture quotations taken from the King James Version (KJV) – *public domain.*

Scripture quotations taken from The Voice Bible (VB) Copyright © 2012 Thomas Nelson, Inc. The Voice™ translation © 2012 Ecclesia Bible Society All rights reserved.

Scripture quotations taken from the Holy Bible, New International Version (NIV). Copyright © 1973, 1978, 1984, 2011 by Biblica, Inc.™. Used by permission. All rights reserved.

Scripture quotations taken from the Amplified Bible (AMP). Copyright © 1954, 1958, 1962, 1964, 1965, 1987 by The Lockman Foundation. Used by permission. All rights reserved.

Paperback ISBN-13: 978-1-66280-520-2

eBook ISBN-13: 978-1-6628-0521-9

DEDICATION

This book is dedicated to my husband, Albert Fernandez. Without your encouragement and support my dream to become a published author would have remained just that; a dream.

Acknowledgements

To my parents, Kenneth and Carole Barker, I love you so much, thank you for supporting me in everything that I do. Without you there would be no me.

To my pastors, Drs. Robert and Sheila Poole, my father and mother in the faith, my BIL and my sister, thank you for pouring into me, I am the better for it.

To Marcy Shannon, you will always be my little sister, thank you for your encouragement and honest feedback.

To my sons Jamar and D'lon, I am so Godly proud of you both and encourage you to continually listen for God's voice and do what He says, you can't go wrong.

To Dr. Grayce James, PhD, thank you for sharing your story and allowing me to share it in these pages. I thank God for our divine connection.

To Josephine Thomas, thank you for being so open and honest with your testimonies, I know many will be blessed by them.

To the Anonymous Child of God, I thank God that our paths have crossed. We thought it was about work, but God had a much bigger plan for the both of us. I am honored to call you my friend. I look forward to having tea with you soon.

TABLE OF CONTENTS

FOREWORD

IT IS VERY DIFFICULT TO HEAR AMID A MULTI-
tude of noises. One must focus on the one speaking to them
and somehow block out as much of the surrounding voices
as possible. Proverbs says in the first chapter that Lady
Wisdom cries above the commotion. It is the responsibility
of the listener to hear what is being said. God is speaking,
always. However, we all too often miss His voice due to the
commotions of everyday life.

In this book Tressa addresses that and so much more to
help us know we're hearing God. As you read this practical,
yet profound work, you will discover just how easy and necessary it is to hear God. You will laugh and perhaps cry as
Tressa shares her testimonies and journey to hearing God
clearly and consistently. By the time you're finished reading
this book, you will not only know God is speaking, you will
be confident in knowing you're hearing Him.

Jesus said on numerous occasions to those who were listening to Him, "He that has an ear to hear let him hear what
the Spirit is saying". I pray you will have ears to hear what
God is saying to you from the pages of this book. More
importantly than hearing, I pray you will be a doer of what

God speaks. God is speaking! Open up your heart to hear clearly what He has to say to you.

Dr. Robert J. Poole, Jr.
Destiny Christian Center

God Is Speaking, Are You Listening was written to encourage believers that God truly is speaking. Tressa has openly and candidly shared her life experiences when God was covering and keeping her before she knew Him. It was in those times she realized after she began serving the Lord that God was in fact "speaking" to her. This book is a must read for those who find themselves struggling to hear and or discern the voice of God.

Her writing style is so warm and inviting, that it will cause you find a comfy chair, and feel as if she is there with you sharing her life's story. As you read this book, you will experience God's peace knowing that He is speaking.

Dr. Sheila Poole
Destiny Christian Center

Introduction

*My sheep hear my voice, and I know
them, and they follow me.*
John 10:27 NKJ

See to it that you do not refuse Him who speaks.
Hebrews 1:25 NKJ

I OFTEN HEAR PEOPLE SAY THAT GOD DOESN'T speak to them. I've said it myself, many times. However, what I've learned over the years is that God is always speaking; the issue is that I don't always listen.

I've also learned that when God speaks, it generally isn't in some deep, booming James Earl Jones-like voice; it's in a variety of ways. My Pastor often says, "God is speaking, and He sounds a lot like your Pastor." God also speaks through scripture, prayer, praise, worship, the testimonies of others, and sometimes, simply through a thought, feeling, or a prompt.

I used to think I wasn't spiritual enough. I have heard many in ministry say that God has spoken to them through very specific and prophetic visions and dreams, telling them deep, wonderful things. I would think, *"Wow, that's never happened to me, I must be too shallow and definitely not spiritual enough because God has never spoken to me in that way."*

God is calling us to listen for Him. In the Bible there are about eighteen scriptures in the New Testament that say, "He that has ears to hear, let him hear." This call is often from Jesus Himself. I challenge you to look it up. It's important. So important that Jesus said it over and over, "He that has ears to hear, let him hear."

The purpose of this book is twofold:

1. To show you through my life experiences and stories of my friends and family, that God is speaking to us; all the time, in many ways no matter where we are in life.
2. To challenge you to listen for His voice. God's sheep hear His voice, and once you hear His voice, take heed and do what He says.

How do you know it's God and not heartburn, your conscience, or even the enemy? Very simple, God will never speak anything that is contrary to His word. That's why it's important for you to read your Bible to know it for yourself and find scriptures to back up anything that you are hearing, be it in your spirit, from your Pastor, friends or family.

I pray that you will be blessed by the stories I have shared in the following chapters. When you are finished, I pray that you will know that God speaks to you, and you'll be determined to not only listen, but to be a doer of the word that you hear.

CHAPTER

1

BEFORE I KNEW HIM

The Lord protects those of childlike faith;
I was facing death, and he saved me.
Let my soul be at rest again, for the
Lord has been good to me.
He has saved me from death, my eyes from tears,
my feet from stumbling.
And so I walk in the Lord's presence as I live
here on earth!
Psalm 116:6-9 NLT

BEFORE I KNEW HIM, PLAIN AND SIMPLE, I WAS a hot mess. I would lie, steal and cheat without hesitation, feeling nothing in my conscience. I was not thinking about salvation, Jesus, or church. My entire life was centered around me, myself, and I.

Jeremiah 29:11 says, "I know the thoughts and plans that I have for you, to give you a future and a hope." By sparing my life from near-death situations, not once, but twice; by showing His mercy upon me when I stole money and was not arrested; by putting an amazing Christian woman in my life to be a mentor and show me what Christian character looks like; God did just that. He gave me a future and a hope.

The point of the following testimonies is whether we know the Lord or not, His hand is upon our lives, He is speaking. Even when I was not listening, He was divinely orchestrating my life in ways I couldn't imagine because I had no awareness of Him. My eyes were veiled, and He was a mystery to me. However, He was always speaking to me, drawing me to His grace, love, and mercy.

A New Mommy

"We need you to sign here, here and here," were the last words I heard as I was whisked off to surgery. I had been in pain all day long, couldn't get comfortable, eat, sleep or do anything; I was just in pain. I finally told my dad I thought something was wrong, and we should go to the hospital. The first thing he wanted to know was if I was in labor. I told him I didn't know. I just knew I was in a lot of pain and something wasn't right. Since I was nine months pregnant, his question was legitimate.

We got to the hospital, and after examination, it was discovered that I had a severe case of toxemia, also known as pre-eclampsia, a blood condition that pregnant women get that causes a sharp rise in blood pressure. It was determined that since I was so far along in the pregnancy and they didn't want the baby to be affected by the toxemia, they would have to induce labor.

Going into labor and having toxemia was scary enough, but the part that I haven't mentioned is that I was only sixteen years old, a child myself. This whole thing was terrifying, and it didn't help that there was someone in labor in another delivery room screaming in agony as if she were about to die.

Labor went on and I was slowly dilating, nearly falling asleep in between contractions, listening to the beep...beep... beep of the monitor that was tracking the baby's heart rate. I awoke instantly when it went to beep, beep, beep, beep, beep. Several nurses rushed into the room, checking monitors, checking me, checking the baby. Then the doctor came in, examined me and determined that the baby was in distress, and they would have to do an emergency C-section. I was rushed off to surgery, signing papers as they were wheeling me down the hall, and next thing I knew, I was asleep.

Jamar Kenneth Barker was born on March 6, 1983, weighing in at six pounds, seven ounces; a beautiful baby boy. However, I was not doing so good. After the surgery, they could not stop the bleeding, and a blood transfusion was required. Which seemed easy enough, except I have rare blood, and they did not have my type of blood at the hospital. They checked several local hospitals, and all the while the bleeding would not stop. They finally found my blood type at a local blood bank.

They did a blood transfusion, and after some time, the bleeding stopped. My family thought I was on the road to recovery, but I would not wake up. The only thing I would respond to was pain. I had been given too much pain medication, and my body couldn't take it. After three days of being unconscious, I finally began to wake up. I can remember feeling as though I was under water, struggling to swim to the surface, to the light, but feeling so weighed down that I couldn't get to the top.

You may be thinking, *"Finally she began the healing process and could get on with her new life as a mother."* Not quite, once I woke up, I had developed an infection. I had to have another surgery to deal with the infection.

I came through the second surgery well. This time, I woke up in the normal time period and began healing. After almost a month in the hospital, I finally went home.

I could have died at any time during that whole ordeal; I could have stroked out due to the extremely high blood pressure from the toxemia, bled to death because they could not stop the bleeding or find my blood type, or never regained consciousness. But God had a plan for me; to give me a future and a hope.

I went on with my life, and this is not the part where I tell you that I realized that I had a near-death experience, saw Jesus, repented, and got saved. Nope, that's not what happened. I went on with my life, oblivious to what God had done for me.

<u>*Fast forward 14 years*</u>

    I was having a serious problem with a cyst in a very delicate area and because of the agonizing pain and location of the cyst, it was determined that I would need to have surgery to remove it. The procedure was scheduled at Valley Hospital, where my mom worked.

    'Tressa...Tressa, can you hear me?" I slowly opened my eyes to the most piercing blue eyes I've ever seen. "Tressa?" As my eyes focused, he said, "Don't try to speak." I began searching the room for a familiar face, my mom, or my fiancé Albert. "Tressa, don't be afraid, you have a tube down your throat and your hands are tied to the bed to prevent you from trying to remove the tube." Immediately, I tried to lift my hands, and just like Mr. Blue Eyes said, my hands were tied to the bed. "Try to relax," came a voice from the right side of the room. *Ahhh I know that voice; mom.* I turned my head, my eyes searching her eyes for answers. "You had a reaction to the antibiotic we gave you during surgery and went into anaphylactic shock, and we almost lost you," said Mr. Blue Eyes. "I'm Dr. Samuelson, I was the anesthesiologist who was in the room during the procedure, and everything was going fine. Dr. Edwards completed the procedure successfully and had left the operating room. We were going through the process of waking you, when within seconds, your throat swelled shut and your heart rate decreased dramatically; then flatlined. We were about to get the paddles when your heart started beating again, and we administered epinephrine into your IV. The only reason you are still with us is because you were intubated."

Anaphylactic shock is a life-threatening allergic reaction that is extremely serious. It can block your airways, prevent you from breathing, and can stop your heart. This is due to the decrease in blood pressure that prevents the heart from receiving enough oxygen.

It is the practice at a hospital when someone is anesthetized that they are intubated, however, it is not the standard practice at an outpatient facility. If I had had the procedure at an outpatient facility, I would not have made it. My throat closed so fast that they wouldn't have had time to cut my throat open and intubate me. The only reason I had the procedure done at a hospital was because of my doctor's schedule. All of his other procedures that day were at the hospital, so instead of scheduling my procedure at an outpatient facility, it was scheduled at the hospital with all of the other procedures he had that day. The hand of the Lord was upon my life that day.

Many that have had a near-death experience say that it must not have been their time to go because they yet had something great to do. Not me, what I realize now is that God spared my life so that I would not burn in hell. I wasn't saved at the time and didn't know God at all. God may still have something great for me to do. But one thing I know for sure, I didn't die that day because God was involved; if I had, because I didn't know Him as my Lord and Savior, I would have gone straight to hell.

I wish I could say that after all that, I got saved. But no, it wasn't until many years later.

Busted

I had a job at a medical center where one of my responsibilities was to make the bank deposits. When I would go to make the bank deposit, I would take some of the money from the deposit and keep it for myself, then make a new deposit slip, and deposit the rest. This went on for about three months, and guess what? The medical center noticed that their money wasn't adding up. I got called in the office, and you can imagine how that conversation went and of course, I was fired. I went on my way, found another job, and went on with my life. About six months later, I was relaxing at home when my phone rang.

"Hello?"

"Is this Tressa Fernandez."

"Yes, it is."

"I'm detective Xavier Parks with the Las Vegas Metropolitan Police Department Investigations Division. I'm calling about an incident that was reported to us by The Medical Center, where they report you stole funds from their deposits, and they want to press charges." My heart was beating so hard that I thought I was going to pass out; the phone became slippery in my hands, and my stomach was in knots. He proceeded to ask me questions about what had happened. He again told me that they wanted to press charges and he would be filing his report and I would hear back from him.

After I got off the phone, I knew that it was over. I was busted, and at any time the police would come knocking on the door and I would be arrested. Days, weeks, months, and years passed. The knock at the door never came. I never heard another word about it. Eighteen years later when I had to pull my police record for a job I was applying for, there was no record of the incident. A report was never filed; charges were never pressed. Once again, I went on with my life, completely oblivious to God's mercy working in my life.

BJC Factor

Barbara Jean Christiansen was my boss at Sierra Health Services for about nine years. She hired me as her secretary when I was twenty something years old. I wasn't the greatest secretary, I mean I did enough to get by, but not one bit more. I took long lunches with my boyfriend and was late for work more than I was on time; my work was mediocre at best.

One day as I was writing an appointment in Barb's calendar, I noticed "T late", written in Barb's neat cursive handwriting at the top of one of the dates. I looked at the week prior and saw it written at the top of three out of the four dates. I flipped back a few more weeks, and there were more notations of "T late". At that moment, my entire work ethic changed. I realized that just because Barb had never said anything, I hadn't gotten away with anything. I owed this woman much more than I had been giving her. I felt like I had really disappointed her, and I had to show her I could do better.

From that day on, I was not late for work again. I took only the allotted hour for lunch, and to the best of my ability I did what I was asked to do, and then some more. I purposed to be the best secretary that I could be. Barbara J. Christiansen was my first exposure to Christian character. I didn't know at the time that she was a Christian, but I had never worked for someone with such integrity. During the nine years that I worked for her, I never saw Barb get angry, I never heard her gossip about anyone. When I would get mad and frustrated with people at work and complain to her about them, she would say, "Kill 'em with kindness Tress, kill 'em with kindness." She was at all of my major life events. I cried on her shoulder when I found out I was pregnant with my second child. She was there when I graduated from college. She was at my wedding and at my twenty-year vow renewal. When my oldest son got hit in the head at school and had to have brain surgery, she came to the hospital and waited with me and my family. Once again, the hand of the Lord was upon my life, shaping me and preparing me for His plan.

God was speaking and moving in my life before I even had a clue about Him. That's what's so amazing about the love of God. He knows all about us and never gives up on us. He patiently waits for us to come to the end of ourselves so He can show us who we were meant to be.

CHAPTER

SALVATION

Then Jesus said, "Come to me, all of you who are weary and carry heavy burdens, and I will give you rest."
Matthew 11:28 NLT

MY SALVATION DID NOT COME AS A RESULT OF some life-changing situation. Although, as you've read in the previous chapter, I had more than one opportunity to do so. It was subtle, I had this emptiness in my life that I tried to fill with partying, sleeping around, and material things; but I continually felt a void. I would cuss, lie, steal, and cheat and I knew it wasn't right. I was one of those people who when asked about salvation would say, "I have my own personal relationship with God." Does that sound familiar? When asked about going to church, my excuse for not going was I didn't want to give my money (a whole

$20 max) to that preacher. I was very concerned that the preacher was going to take my $20 and do who knows what with it.

What led me to a relationship with the Lord was the recurring thought that I had done many, many things that I *knew* going into them that they were bad, wrong, illegal and could hurt me or other people; but I did them anyway without hesitation. Why wouldn't I try something that I knew was good for me, could help me, and make me a better person?

In 2000, my mom and I started going to church, and from the moment I did the Holy Spirit touched me in ways I can't explain. It didn't take long for me to answer the altar call and pray the prayer of salvation. I still had many questions, I was nervous and fearful, but I knew what I was doing was right. I had never felt better about anything I had done in my life.

From that time, my life began to change. I didn't want to do the things I used to do. I didn't want to lie anymore, I didn't want to cuss, steal, or cheat anymore. When I did do those things, I felt such conviction. These changes happened gradually over time, but changes for the better were constantly happening in my life.

About a year after I answered the altar call, I stopped going to church because I was offended. The church was so big, I had so many questions, and I wasn't connected. I felt like a person in the congregation, not a part of the church.

Then God moved in a way that has changed my life forever. My sister Sheila and brother-in-love (aka BIL) Robert
had been living in St. Louis for a number of years. Sheila
had gotten saved in 1987 and Robert in 1989. In St. Louis,
they had been faithful members of their church, but their
ultimate desire was to come back to Las Vegas and start their
own ministry. While they were there, Sheila and I would
talk, sometimes those conversations ended not-so-great,
with Sheila being frustrated with my lack of desire to get to
know God. I was convinced that it just didn't take all of that,
and thought they were way too spiritual. Sometimes when
we talked, I would ask her questions about Christianity and
the Bible. We would have great conversations, but when the
conversation was over, I would go back to my life, and she
would go back to hers.

The last two times when Sheila and Robert left to return
home after visiting Vegas, we felt so sad; Sheila didn't want
to leave, and I didn't want her to go. Our sons were about
the same age and they along with their daughter were all
getting to know each other and had a great time together.

It wasn't long after that last time they visited when
Sheila called me and told me they were moving back to
Vegas. Not only were they coming home, but they were
going to start a church, and it was going to be called Destiny
Christian Center. I knew from the moment she told me
they were starting a church, that I would be a part of whatever they were doing. It was solidified on February 5, 2001,
when I heard my BIL minister for the first time. It was like

God was speaking directly to me saying, "To Tressa, Love God." When I heard my sister preach for the first time, I was blown away. I had known this person all of her life and had no idea this was in her. When she and Robert minister, they do it with such passion; it is so clear that they want you to get it. They have taught me how to read my Bible, how to pray, and how to develop a relationship with God. They are my Pastors, my father and mother in the faith, and I thank God for them. I am convinced that it was my sister's prayers that drew me to God.

God speaks to me through them on a regular basis, and I strive to follow after them as they follow Christ. The more that I follow after them, the more I hear God speak, and the more I am learning to be obedient to what God is calling me to do.

I now teach New Member's class at Destiny Christian Center and when talking about how I came to Destiny, I tell people that God knew that I needed special help in my walk with the Lord. How he divinely arranged for Pastors Robert and Sheila Poole to come back to Vegas and start the church so that I could learn of Him and connect with people that I knew, could relate to and learn from. I truly feel the heart and love of God through my Pastors and look forward to continuing to hear God speak through them.

CHAPTER

3

PROVERBS 31 WOMAN

Her husband can trust her,
and she will greatly enrich his life.
She brings him good, not harm, all the days
of her life.
Proverbs 31:11-12 NLT

I HAD DONE IT AGAIN, SPENT MORE MONEY than was in the checking account. The rent was late, bills were past due, and I had no explanation. What could I tell my husband that would fix it? "I'm sorry" or, "I won't do it again"? These were all words that had been spoken before, with sincerity at the time, until it happened again.

"Babe, I don't understand how this is happening, why won't you talk with me about what's going on with the money?" Al said. My husband is a man of few words, and the words he spoke that day were sharp, painful, and true. I got defensive, which led to getting mad. I went to bed that night crying, frustrated, and angry.

I woke up the next day with lingering feelings of anger, thinking that I had a few more things to say about how he wasn't all that perfect. In my mind I began developing a list of his faults and what I thought he should do to fix them.

Fueled by what I was going to put on the list, I went into my craft room and signed on to the computer. The list was going to start with the last time he had stayed out all night and had me worried sick. I opened my email and did a quick scan of what was new. I clicked on the *Proverbs 31 Woman Devotional.* I read the text and stopped when I read: Proverbs 31:11, *Her husband can trust her, and she will greatly enrich his life.*

Can Al trust you? What are you doing to enrich his life?

The words resonated in my mind. Right then, the anger drained out of me. I was hit hard with the fact that Al could not trust me, and my poor management of our finances was not enriching his life, my life, or our life together. He could not trust me to pay the bills at all, let alone on time. He could not trust me to communicate with him what was going on, he could not trust me to do what I said I was going to do with our finances. He could not trust me, period.

What had started out as a list of his faults, turned into a list of what I needed to do to regain his trust with our finances. I began to pray and asked God to forgive me and to help me to be a wife that my husband could trust.

When he came home from work that night, I apologized for making a mess of our finances and committed to him that I would do better. I showed him a budget that I had created. At first, he was skeptical; we had been down this road before. However, I acknowledged God in the situation and asked Him to guide my footsteps and direct my path. I started paying bills on time, and Al and I met weekly so I could keep him apprised of what was going on with our finances. We determined what bills I would be responsible for and those that he would be responsible for.

Over the next several months, I went out of my way to show my husband that he could trust me. And over time he began to do just that. Our weekly meetings are no longer necessary because he now has confidence in me that the bills are getting paid on time; he trusts me, and I go out of my way to enrich his life.

It's funny that sometimes when God speaks, I respond immediately with change. But not always. Like all of us, I am a work in progress growing to the place where every time God speaks, I listen and am obedient right away, all the way, and with the right attitude.

CHAPTER

4

WHO ARE YOU?

"For I know the plans I have for you," says the Lord.
"They are plans for good and not for disaster,
to give you a future and a hope.
Jeremiah 29:11 NLT

I WALKED OUT OF THE NEW VICE PRESIDENT'S
office thinking, *"I've got to find another job because this man
is going to fire me."*

For the first time in my professional career, I had gotten
written up, accused of not doing my job properly. The vice
president stated that he had "counseled" me, and I hadn't
responded, and he had repeatedly asked me for a report,
and I hadn't given it to him. The "counseling" he had done
was he had given me a book on contract negotiation a few
weeks prior and recommended that I read it. "You're a nice

person, and you do good things, but I ask myself if that's enough," he'd said in the meeting.

I left his office and returned to my desk, knowing that I needed to start looking for a new job A.S.A.P. In the ensuing weeks I was left out of negotiation meetings on contracts that I had been the lead on. There was no attempt to veil the fact that I was being squeezed out. Nothing like this had ever happened to me before. Since the BJC factor, I had enjoyed favorable bosses, awesome mentors, professional relationships, and excellent performance reviews.

I had been the Manager of Network Development for two years and had worked at the Culinary Health Fund a total of six years. I had come a long way from my humble beginnings in health care as a secretary for Barb Christiansen. I had gone to school and gotten my bachelor's degree in business management. I was comfortable in my job and making good money. I had been recruited to this job by my current manager. I hadn't had to actively look for a job in over ten years.

As I sat there in my office with all of these thoughts whirling around in my head, I was dreading the process of job-hunting, and anxiety began to well up in me. "Lord, what am I going to do?" I thought. Then the "what if's" started: What if I can't find a job making the same kind of money, what if I can't find a job at all?

I kept thinking of the VP's words, "You're a nice person and you do good things, but I have to ask myself, is that enough?" What was he saying? What did he mean by that? Then a thought hit me.

This job does not define who you are.

That was a powerful statement. I was surrounded by people whose career defined who they were; it was all about their education, their position, their salary. Many sacrifices had been made for the sake of the job. Long hours, time away from family; all for the sake of the job. Again, the thought:

This job, any job you have, does not define who you are, it is merely a resource.

After that, I had peace about leaving that job. The understanding that my title did not define me, it didn't validate me, it didn't do anything but provide me with a resource to be able to take care of my financial obligations was so freeing to me. It didn't matter if the new VP thought I was good enough. It only mattered that God thought I was good enough, and He had a plan for me that had nothing to do with my career path or job title.

As I continued to think about this, I went to the scriptures, and the truth of that statement became clearer to me. Romans 8:37, I am more than a conqueror; 2 Corinthians 5:17, I am a new creation in Christ; Revelations 12:11, I am an overcomer; 1 Corinthians 15:57, I am victorious through Christ Jesus.

The more I read the scriptures, the more I understood who I was in Christ, and I was at peace with what was to come. It is so easy to lose focus and get caught up in what other people, society, friends, family or even what you think defines you. Once I knew who God said I was, I took great comfort in that. I was able to move forward with the job-hunting process, work in peace with people that I knew were against me, and trust God to open doors for me that no man could shut.

Chapter

5

YOU ARE NOT THE BREADWINNER

For the husband is the head of the wife,
even as Christ is the head of the church:
and he is the Savior of the body.
Ephesians 5:23 KJ

"YOUR BASE SALARY WILL BE $45,000 ANNU-ally, with commission based on the number of doctors that start using LabCorp and the number of tests they order," said the recruiter that called to offer me the job. That was a pretty significant cut from the nearly $75,000 annually that I was making at the Culinary Health Fund. An account executive was a completely different type of job for me, but it was time to leave the Culinary Health Fund. I knew that they were going to try to get rid of me, and I wanted to be ahead of them and leave on my own terms. I had been working in health care contracting for nineteen years. If I was going to switch jobs, I wanted to do something different. But a 25% cut in pay? The recruiter did say there would be commission that would average about what I was making at the Culinary Health Fund, and there was potential to make more than that. I took the job, and guess what? The commission average wasn't even close to what my salary had been at the previous job.

I stressed and fretted about how I (notice, I) was going to make ends meet. All of this while I drove around using a company vehicle that I could drive for my own personal use, including going out of town. I didn't have to pay for not one drop of gas during a time when gas was over $4 a gallon! Oh how God provided for me! But I continued to try to figure out how I was going to make up for the reduction in my salary. Bills started to get behind, and the more they got behind, the more I got angry with LabCorp. They had lied, the whole commission program was bogus! On top of that, they wanted me to pay for client lunches and then submit my receipts for reimbursement, which sometimes took two to three months! I was pissed, and all the while trying to figure out how I was going to make ends meet.

One day as I was again worrying about how bills were going to get paid, the thought crossed my mind:

What about Al?

"What about him?" Was my immediate thought.

What about his business?

"What about it?" I thought and went on with my day.

Later that week I came across the book *The Power of A Praying Wife* by Stormie O'Martian (Coincidence? I think not). In that book, I found a prayer to pray for my husband's work. That's when it clicked. *What about Al? What about his business?* I had prayed for my husband's business before, but now it occurred to me to not only pray for his business, but specifically pray for his business to increase, for his business to bring in enough to take care of our household needs.

There was a thought. My income was never intended to take care of our household needs. I am not the breadwinner. Could I believe God that whatever I make would be extra, over and above? This was a big revelation for me. I had the revelation that because I had been a single mother for fourteen years before I got married, and if I didn't make it happen, it didn't happen. However, now that I was married, that was no longer the case. That had not been the case for about six years. I had been so conditioned to "be the breadwinner" but now, God was showing me something different. To first of all trust Him, and second of all, I was out of order trying to figure out how I was going to make ends meet. Not that it was all up to my husband, but more that I needed to pray for him and believe God to allow my husband to be the leader, the priest of our home. God was bigger than my situation and could move on my husband's behalf due to my prayers, and all of our needs would be met according to His riches in Christ Jesus.

As I began to refocus my prayers, you know what happened? All of our needs were met. God provided for my husband's business and it grew, he grew, and I became closer to my husband through prayer. It caused me to take the focus off of me and turn it toward my husband, and our marriage. I didn't lean on LabCorp for provision, but my Lord and Savior, who knew what I had need of. I needed to trust Him and lean not to my own understanding. One thing I've learned in this Christian walk is that I have to be willing to look at myself honestly, and when I hear God speak, listen and be willing to change.

CHAPTER

6

THE JOB AT THE CITY

*Trust in The Lord with all your heart and lean not
to your own understanding.
In all your ways acknowledge Him, and He shall
direct your paths.*
Proverbs 3:5 NKJ

*For the Lord will be your confidence,
and He will keep your foot from being caught.*
Proverbs 3:26 NKJ

ONCE I REALIZED IT WAS TIME TO MOVE ON
from LabCorp, I again began the dreaded task of looking
for a job. I had begun the process of updating my resume
and started putting some feelers out there. During this time,
my uncle passed away suddenly.

At his funeral I saw a friend of the family, who I hadn't seen in a long time. I had babysat for her many years ago, when I was about sixteen years old. As we got to chatting, she told me that she was now the Director of HR at the City of Las Vegas. I told her that I had been thinking that I needed a career change and had been looking into working for the government. She gave me her card and told me to give her a call sometime.

About a month later I took her up on her offer, and we set up a meeting. At the meeting we talked about my education, my experience, and what I might like to do at the City. She said at the time, there were no positions open. She told me that I should watch the website and if anything that interested me came up to give her a call, and she would pass on my resume to a few people that she knew.

We talked about a couple of departments that my skill set would be a match for, and she mentioned that the Purchasing and Contracts Division would have an opening soon. Since my background was in contracting, it sounded interesting to me. "As I think about it, that's a difficult department to work in, you wouldn't want to work there," she told me. "Besides, they would be looking for someone with experience working for the government." We talked about some other possible openings, and that I would potentially have to take a job with less pay than I was currently making because of my lack of experience in the field. I let her know that I was aware that would be part of transitioning into a new field, and I was ok with it.

Time went by and I regularly checked the City's webpage to see what opportunities were available. A couple of months later there it was, a posting for a Contracts Specialist in the Purchasing and Contracts Division. There was also a position for a secretary in another department. I was so excited I applied for both positions and couldn't wait to let my HR connection know.

When I called her and told her I'd applied for the Contracts Specialist position, she immediately said, "Oh, they probably won't even consider you because they are looking for someone with government contracting experience. But I will talk to the person that is hiring for the secretary position."

I was a bit deflated, but thought, *"Oh well, I already submitted the application for the job, so we'll see what happens."* About a month later, I got a call from the HR department to schedule an interview for the Contracts Specialist position. It was a three-hour interview; the longest interview I have ever had. It started with a panel of the management team, then a panel of the staff that I would be working with. After it was over, they informed me that no matter how long it took, don't call them; that I would receive an email from Human Resources to let me know the outcome of the interview. It took what seemed like an eternity for the City to contact me. My phone rang as I was driving to an appointment about a month later.

"Hello, is this Tressa Fernandez?"

"Yes, it is."

"This is Marlon Thompson with the City of Las Vegas; I'm calling regarding the Contracts Specialist position. I know it has been a while, if you are still interested in the position, we would like to make you an offer."

"Yes, I sure am interested!"

Marlon went on to tell me the rest of the details of the position, we agreed on a start date and when I hung up the phone, I thanked God and cried I was so happy. About a month after I started the job, I was attending a City Council meeting with my new boss, where we encountered my HR connection.

"Hello," said my boss, "I would like to introduce you to Tressa Fernandez our newest Contract Specialist."

"I've known Tressa for many years, since she was a teenager," she said, "I was going to give her resume to the Planning Department for the secretary position."

"She's with Purchasing now, and Planning can't steal her away, we have big plans for her!" my boss said.

"That's great, Tressa, I'm glad you're now a part of the City team," my HR connection said.

The Holy Spirit ministered to me right then and there. I didn't need someone to "juice" me into the City. I didn't need the favor of my HR connection. God made it very clear that she had nothing to do with my getting the job. She had come right out and said that Purchasing wouldn't be interested in hiring me because of my lack of experience, but God had another plan! He knows the thoughts and plans He has for me to give me a future and a hope and does not need my help in carrying out His plans for my life.

CHAPTER
7

THE MELTDOWN

It's clear that our flesh entices us into practicing
some of its most heinous acts:
...arguing,...anger, selfishness,
contentiousness, division,
Galatians 5:19-20 The Voice Bible

IT HAD BEEN A REALLY LONG DAY, I HAD TO take my grandkids home to Henderson, NV and then go to a leadership meeting at the Pastor's house, about an hour and thirty-minute drive round trip. At the leadership meeting the Pastor had brought correction. During the meeting my phone rang; I had forgotten to send my grandson's seizure medication home with him, so I had to leave the staff meeting and drive back to Henderson to take the medicine to my grandson. On the drive home, I was so frustrated and angry and had gotten myself all worked up.

During the drive I had decided that when I got home, I was going to talk to Al. It could not wait any longer. I needed to know what the deal was that he wasn't saved. I wanted him to explain to my why he thought salvation was great for me and our son D'lon but not for him.

You should pray before talking to Al.

I brushed that thought away and decided that this needed to get dealt with right now. When I got home, I went into the bedroom and changed clothes, all the while getting myself more and more worked up as I thought about how much better things would be if he was saved. In my mind we were unequally yoked. I couldn't talk to him about spiritual things and who knew what he was not sharing with me because he thought I was too spiritual.

When he came into the room, I laid it on him. "Babe, we need to talk. What is it exactly that is holding you back from getting saved?"

"What are you talking about?" he said.

"I want to know where you are with God. You think it's great for me and D'lon, but what about you? Do you ever think about your relationship with Christ?"

"No, I don't think about it, and I don't want to talk about it right now." Then he turned around and walked out of the room.

I was stunned. *He didn't even think about it.* I burst into tears. I hadn't expected him to refuse to talk about it. Never in the twenty-eight years that we'd known each other, in all of the disagreements we had, he had never refused to talk.

I cried until I had no more tears, feeling like never had he shut me out so completely. Did this mean he had no intention of getting saved? Lord, how is this going to work? How could we be together if he doesn't want anything to do with God? The word "divorce" flashed through my mind.

That thought shook me to my core, and I snapped out of my teary haze.

I told you to pray before you talked to him.

Ah, but I had been full-blown in my emotions, and completely ignored that thought.

I wiped my face, got my Bible and looked up what God intended marriage to be. Dr. Poole had just taught us in Bible study that week that everything starts in Genesis, so I went there and found Genesis 2:24: *"Therefore a man shall leave his father and mother and be joined to his wife, and they shall become one flesh."* They shall become one flesh. Therefore, if we're one flesh, divorce is not possible.

"Lord if divorce is not possible, then why would You have me get saved and not my husband?" I thought. Fresh tears streamed down my face. I got out my iPad and Googled "Prayer for unsaved husband" and found *8 Steps to Living Peaceably With Your Unsaved Husband,* a blog post written by Kate Plourde. It was as if she had written this just for me! The thing that stood out to me the most was:

> *"Another reason to stay married to your husband is for the children. This same verse (1 Corinthians 7:14) says children living with a Christian*

> *parent are holy rather than unclean. Therefore,*
> *remember that your presence in their lives is of*
> *great influence."*

Because of my salvation, our son D'lon got saved when he was eight years old and was growing up in the love of God. He was being trained in the way that he should go. He was learning about God and developing a relationship with Him at a young age, which already put him years before me; I didn't come to know the Lord until in my thirties. Even if Al never came to know the Lord, our son knew God and had a relationship with Him, and for that I was eternally thankful!

I went on to pray for my husband and our marriage. I knew that I should not have had that conversation with Al without praying and seeking the Lord first. I repented for my behavior. I had caught my husband off guard asking him about salvation, I didn't give him any preface, just wham! That's what happens when you let your emotions lead and your flesh talk!

God spoke and led me to pray for my marriage the scriptures referenced in *8 Steps to Living Peaceably With Your Unsaved Husband* which helped me to trust God's divine plan for my husband, our marriage, and our family.

I've discovered it's not for me to get my husband saved. My job is to pray for him, to live upright before him, and show him the love of God at every opportunity. I have not asked my husband about being saved since then and will not unless the Holy Spirit tells me to. I pray for his salvation regularly and trust and believe God to do the rest.

CHAPTER
8

THE GREATEST TEST
OF MY FAITH

So Jesus answered and said to them,
"Have faith in God."
Mark 11:22 NKJ

I PULLED UP TO THE CURB AND MY SON JAMAR got out of the car, taking his 9-month-old son Alex with him.

This was not how it was supposed to be. I drove off, leaving them on the sidewalk, looking back at them getting smaller and smaller in the rear-view mirror. With tears pouring down my face, I left them there and did not see or hear from them for over a year.

The scene earlier had not been pretty. My son Jamar and his baby's mama Denise had been fighting. He wanted me to talk to her, and I had nothing to say. I was smack dab in the middle of their drama, all for the sake of my grandson. I wanted to be like the storybook grandma, but we were not off to a good start.

"Mom, will you just talk to her?"

"I'm not the one who slept with her and had a baby with her." I said to Jamar as my phone was ringing and ringing and ringing. She would keep calling until I answered. I finally answered, and the exchange of words was not pretty. I hung up and immediately the phone started ringing again.

I pulled away from the curb that day, leaving my son and grandson behind, went to the phone company and had my phone number changed.

That night I slept peacefully, completely experiencing Philippians 4:6-7 (NLT), "Don't worry about anything, instead pray about everything. Tell God what you need and thank Him for all He has done. Then you will experience God's peace, which exceeds anything we can understand. His peace will guard your hearts and minds as you live in Jesus Christ."

Initially Jamar and Alex were at my house for just one night, that turned into a week, and then another week. Tension was rising on every side. Arguments took place every time Jamar and Denise talked. Jamar would disappear and leave us with the baby for days at a time. Al tried to be patient, but his patience was running out. The final blow was when Jamar disappeared for several days, Alex got sick with the flu, and Al and I ended up with the flu. I mean it was bad, coming out of both ends type of flu. I knew that

Jamar had to go, but they had nowhere to go. I didn't know what to do.

Do you trust me?

"Of course," was my immediate response.

Do you trust me with your son and your grandson? Do you believe that I can help them?

Did I trust God? The cinema in my mind began to roll the film of all the times I had run to Jamar's rescue. All the times I had tried to "fix" the situation, knowing that it was not the right thing to do. Things like getting he and Denise's power bill in my name when they were living together. I knew that wasn't right, they were fornicating! But I wanted to help. Buying food, diapers, doing anything I could to help. I wanted to be the storybook grandma. But this was no fairytale. If I trusted God, why was I always trying to do something?

The more I thought about it, the more I realized that the answer to the question was no; I did not trust God. My actions clearly displayed that I thought I could do a better job than God could. After all, this was my son and grandson.

Then what was I to do? My natural reaction was to say that I didn't know what to do. But I knew exactly what to do; find scriptures about the situation and pray those scriptures. Ask God to help me to trust Him and not run after Jamar every time he got into a situation (a.k.a. lean to my own understanding).

So that's exactly what I did. I prayed that God would protect Jamar and especially Alex. That was the really hard part about the situation. This innocent nine-month-old child, who had no control over who his parents were and had no control over this situation. More than anything, that was why I was reacting, that was why I wanted to "fix" it; for the sake of my grandson. I learned the hard way, over and over again, that I could not fix it. I had to trust God in the situation and understand that the power was in the praying, the power was having faith in God to protect and take care of Jamar and Alex.

Jamar has been the greatest test of my faith. I have had to come to the hard conclusion that each time I dropped everything and bent over backwards to help him, not only was I enabling him, I was showing God that I did not trust Him.

I had only been saved a couple of years when all this was happening, but I went to the Bible to find help. I'm not even really sure how I did it, but during this time is when I memorized my first scripture, Philippians 4:6-7. "Be anxious for nothing but in everything with prayer and supplication with thanksgiving, let your requests be made known to God; and the peace of God, which surpasses all understanding will guard your hearts and mind through Christ Jesus." When I put this scripture into practice, I stopped worrying about Jamar and his situation and every-thing that was going on with him, and instead made my requests known to God. I prayed for Jamar to accept the Lord as His Savior, to stand up and be a man, and to deal with his problems, for God to protect him while he was out there figuring it all out, and mainly, for him to protect my grandson. I thanked God in advance for doing it, and something amazing happened. I experienced the peace of God. When I truly leaned into God and believed it when I said yes, that I had faith in Him and trusted Him with Jamar and my grandson, His peace flooded over me because I knew He would never leave them or forsake them. I knew I had to continue praying, not run after Jamar and be all caught up in his drama. That is how I was able to leave my son and grandson on the curb at my son's friend's house, drive away, and go to sleep that night with complete and total faith that God would take care of them.

It has taken me a long time to learn this lesson. This was just one of many more times that my faith in God regarding Jamar would be tested. God has had to speak to me several more times over the years; but as I've learned about God and continually trusted Him, I've been able to hear Him when He spoke and do what He said to do.

CHAPTER

9

FORGIVING DENISE

But I say to you, love your enemies,
bless those who curse you,
do good to those who hate you,
and pray for those who spitefully
use you and persecute you,
Matthew 5:44 NKJ

And whenever you stand praying,
if you have anything against anyone, forgive him,
that your Father in heaven may also forgive you
your trespasses.
Mark 11:25 NKJ

I WANTED TO BE TO DENISE LIKE DOROTHY, Jamar's grandmother, was to me when I was a young mother and didn't have a clue. I was ready to support her and teach her, I wanted to be a good grandmother.

However, whenever I helped it seemed like it resulted in more drama. I don't do drama and Jamar and Denise were constant drama. They moved in together, I got the power in my name, my sister gave them a bedroom set, we all helped in any way we could. However, the fighting continued, and eventually Jamar moved out. When he left, he left all of his belongings behind. Denise would not allow him back into the apartment to get his things, so we had to get the police to go over there with us to get it. As we sat in the car waiting for the police to arrive, her brother approached the car and threatened us, I was terrified. Once we got in the apartment, Denise cussed me out so bad that I cannot repeat what was said. We managed to get most of Jamar's things, and he moved in with a friend. Then the games began with being able to see the baby.

I was hurt. I was so angry with both of them. An innocent child in the middle of so much chaos. I had so much animosity toward Denise. Every time I thought about her, Jamar, Alex and the whole messed up situation, I would feel physically ill and get pissed off. One day as I was venting to my sister about something that Denise had done, she interrupted me and said, "You know you have to forgive Denise, right?" I knew that I did, however, I didn't want to. I was still so mad; my heart was broken. I didn't know when I would see my grandson again. In my mind they had ruined everything that being a grandmother should be. Having a relationship with Denise, like the one I'd had with Dorothy was out of the question.

"You know you have to pray for her." Sheila's words pierced through my thoughts.

"Pray for her? No way, not gonna do it."

"The Bible says in Matthew 5:44, "But I say to you, love your enemies and pray for those who persecute you," she said.

I was digging in my heels and thinking how I did not want to pray for this person, when I heard the Holy Ghost very clearly:

What if you are the only person praying for Denise? What if you are the person that I want to pray for Denise? Are you too mad? I forgave you.

Immediately, the anger drained out of me. God had forgiven me and shown me grace and mercy in more ways than I could count, and I knew that I did not deserve any of it. I knew that my salvation was a result of people praying for me.

So, I began to pray for Denise. At first, they were very short prayers; often through clenched teeth. The pain was still very raw, but I couldn't get past the thought that if I didn't pray maybe there was no one else praying for her. That helped me get over myself, and I found scriptures to pray. I prayed for her salvation; I prayed that God would take the anger away. I prayed that whatever it was that caused her to be so angry, God would help her to deal with it. My Pastor says that praying brings you closer to God and closer to the one you are praying for. God began to soften my heart toward Denise. I'm not saying there was a love fest or anything, and initially I didn't pray for her regularly. However, over time I began to pray for her more often, and I had more empathy toward her.

About two years later, Denise called me and told me that she had a job interview coming up and I was the only professional person that she knew. She wanted my advice on what to wear. She let me know that the kids were doing well (somehow in between the fussing and fighting they had another child) and that she wanted them to get baptized. I asked her about her relationship with the Lord. I ministered to her and asked her if she believed in God and wanted to get saved. She said she believed in God, but not right now. I didn't press the issue. When we got off the phone, I heard a soft voice in my spirit, *"What if you had stayed mad?"* It brought me to tears. If I had stayed mad, I would not have had the opportunity to share the Gospel with Denise. No, she didn't get saved, but God reminded me that one man plants another man waters, but God gets the increase.

That was about twelve years ago. God has truly answered my prayers and Denise has come around. She and Jamar had another child, Robert and she allows us see them regularly. We've been able to talk and there were still a lot of rough times between her and Jamar, but she has been respectful to me, and we have built a relationship.

In November 2019, I got a phone call from Denise, crying and hysterical telling me that Jasmine, her sixteen-year-old daughter had run away, and she did not know what to do. I prayed with her and consoled her the best I could and told her I would be over to pick up the kids so she could focus on looking for Jasmine.

I got off the phone, praying and knowing Denise needed the Lord in order to be able to get through this situation. I typed up some scriptures and decided that I was going to minister to her again.

My mom and I went over to her house and I talked to Denise, shared the scriptures with her and led her through the prayer of salvation, we prayed, we cried, and God got the glory. I hugged Denise tight and she hugged me back. It brought even more tears to my eyes because I remembered the first time that I hugged Denise, many years ago, she didn't hug me back and how here we were, in the middle of a crisis and she got saved. Hallelujah!

Many times, the Holy Spirit has asked me, "What If you hadn't prayed? What if you had stayed mad?" God has been up to something for the past fifteen years, and I can't wait to see how it all turns out!

CHAPTER
10

PRAYING D'LON

And in a similar way, the Holy Spirit
takes hold of us in our human
frailty to empower us in our weakness.
For example, at times we don't even
know how to pray,
or know the best things to ask for.
But the Holy Spirit rises up within us
to super-intercede on our behalf,
pleading to God with emotional sighs too deep
for words.
Romans 8:26 TPT

A CYST, IN THE MOST DELICATE AREA IMAGIN-
able, again. My son D'lon took me to urgent care so that I
could get it taken care of. This had happened many times,
and I knew the routine. The doctor was nice, a woman,

which is always helpful when you have these things. She numbed it, cut it, drained it, and whew, instant relief.

She sent me on my way with a prescription for antibiotics and pain. On the way to the pharmacy, I noticed I was feeling really wet. By the time we got home, I could feel moisture soaking through my clothes. I went in my room, took off my clothes, and blood ran down my legs. I got in the tub and tried to put pressure on it, but it was incredibly painful and bleeding so much, I could barely stand to touch it. I was so scared because I have had multiple cysts over the years, and there had never been so much blood. I freaked out and called D'lon and told him to call his dad. I was crying and getting more and more upset, not knowing what to do because there was just so much blood! D'lon called my husband, who was at work in the middle of a job but said he would come right away. In the meantime, I was still standing in the tub crying, on the verge of hysteria when I heard words, in a language I didn't understand, coming from my bedroom. It was D'lon. He was down on one knee, with his back to me, praying in tongues. Instantly I was calmed. I stopped crying and started thinking, I had D'lon call the urgent care office. I talked to the nurse who explained that the reason it was bleeding so much was because the doctor hadn't packed the incision with gauze to minimize the bleeding. She said I could come back to the urgent care and get it done, but it would be really painful. She told me to apply pressure to it and the bleeding should stop. So, I sucked it up and applied as much pressure as I could stand. By that time Al had come home and helped me out of the tub and into bed, where I continued to put pressure on it, and before long the pain meds kicked in and I fell asleep.

In a moment of panic, God ministered to me though my seventeen-year-old son. Hearing him praying allowed me to regain my composure so I could deal with the situation and calm down enough to get help.

CHAPTER

11

THE TEST CONTINUES

Beloved, do not be surprised at the fiery ordeal
which is taking place to test you
(that is to test the quality of your faith),
as though something strange or unusual were
happening to you.
1 Peter 4:12 AMP

THE PHONE RANG, INTERRUPTING MY PRAYER
time, seeing it was my mom I answered it. That was my
first mistake.

"Hey mom."

"Hi, what are you doing?"

"Not too much, just some things around the house,"
I replied.

We went on to talk about a variety of things. She hadn't
wanted anything in particular, she chatted about what was

going on in her day and asked about what I would be doing in my day.

As we were wrapping up the conversation, she asked, "Did you know that Jamar was back in town?" The question caught me off guard, because as far as I knew he had gone back to Victorville at least a week ago. "Back where, in Vegas?" I said.

"Yes."

"Living here?"

"I guess, I don't know."

"Where is he staying?"

"Well the last I heard he was at your Aunt Marilyn's house," she said.

He had lied to me again. My heart started pounding in my ears, and a knot formed in my stomach.

"This was about two weeks ago, I haven't heard anything since then, so I really don't know if he's still here," she said.

"I did know that he was here about two weeks ago, but he was only supposed to be here a couple of days," I said.

I was done talking and got off the phone with my mom. The thoughts continued running through my mind. I couldn't believe it; he didn't go back to California. The reason he said he was coming out to Vegas was to help with a situation going on with Alex in court. After a phone call to Denise, I found out they didn't even go to court. I began to cry; I had been duped by Jamar again. I was mad. I wondered if he was still clean. I would just be sick if I was a part to him going back to drugs and drinking because I bought him the bus ticket back to Vegas. I knew the answer to the question. Why else would he tell such an elaborate lie? With tears streaming down my face and all kinds of scenarios swirling through my head, the Holy Spirit reminded me of what I had read just days earlier during my devotional time.

In Leviticus 10:1-7 Aaron's sons had burned incense in the tabernacle at the incorrect time and in the incorrect way and God struck them dead. God did not allow Aaron one moment to mourn the death of His sons. Aaron had to continue on with what God had called him to do in the tabernacle. I did not have time to shed one more tear over Jamar. I had to do what God had called me to do, which is pray. I was reminded once again that it doesn't matter how I feel. I shouldn't have answered the phone when my mom called; I should have stayed focused on what I was supposed to be doing which was praying.

I dried up the tears and began to pray for my son. I prayed that he would be able to resist the temptation to drink or do drugs, declaring that greater is the Lord who is in him, than the enemy who is in this world trying to take him out. As I prayed, the anxiousness faded away, my heart rate returned to normal, and I concluded that it didn't matter if Jamar was still in Las Vegas or not. What I needed to do is remain prayerful and focus on God.

God reminded me of what He said in His word, and I listened; dried up the tears, and got busy praying.

12

WORKING FOR
PHARAOH IN EGYPT

*...Train these young men in the language
and literature of Babylon.*
Daniel 1:4 NLT

*God gave these four young men an unusual
aptitude for understanding
every aspect of literature and wisdom.
And God gave Daniel the special
ability to interpret the meanings of visions
and dreams.*
Daniel 1:17 NLT

I HAVE TO BE AT WORK AT 7:00 A.M. MONDAY
through Thursday. I've had this schedule for at least six

years. If I want to spend at least an hour with God before I go to work, I have to get up at about 4:45 a.m. Over the years, I have struggled with getting up on time, and when I do get up on time, that time goes by so fast. Part of my devotion time included reading the Bible through in a year, where each day I read scriptures from the Old and New Testament, the Psalms and Proverbs. I was left feeling like I was rushing through my time with God and worse, shorting my time with God if I woke up late.

My sister, on the other hand, is a Pastor in full-time ministry. Often when we would talk, I would feel envious because she would have long wonderful times of devotion with the Lord. She didn't have to get up at a specific time to pray, and since she didn't have a specific time to be at a job, her prayer time could vary. If she needed to spend more time with the Lord, she could.

She would call me at work filling me in on what she was doing throughout the day, which often involved, what I'll call, non-ministry related activities. There I'd be sitting at work, multi-tasking while talking to her and often hanging up to go to a meeting or deal with a crisis. I believed that she could not relate to the work-life-ministry balance because she didn't have the work piece to balance. The work piece seemed to be such a big piece of my life, ten-hour chunks of the day, Monday through Thursday and spending off days catching up with everything else from household management and ministry responsibilities.

There also were several women in the ministry that were blessed to not have to work, and again, I was a bit envious and felt that they could pretty much spend as much time with the Lord as they wanted before having to start their day. Notice, I didn't account for the fact that all of these women had children that they had to tend to, while my children are grown. But we won't go into that right now.

When my sister would tell me things that she would go through in a day, I could not relate to her, and she could not relate to me, because most of what she does focuses around ministry. She works with her husband (the Pastor) every day and most of the people that she deals with are Christians.

On the other hand, each day off I went to work (Egypt) to deal with my boss (Pharaoh) and my co-workers. I was transitioning into a new position which required me to learn a lot more about local government law, which is boring stuff to read and takes a special skill to comprehend.

One morning as I was reading in the book of Daniel the Holy Spirit ministered to me and I was blessed beyond measure. It pretty much changed my life.

Daniel 1:9, "Now God had given the chief of staff both respect and affection for Daniel." Daniel 1:17, "God gave these four young men an unusual aptitude for understanding every aspect of literature and wisdom. And God gave Daniel the special ability to interpret the meanings of visions and dreams."

Daniel had a crazy boss that made unreasonable demands on him and the people he worked with. Still Daniel prayed, the Lord gave him favor, and those who worked for Pharaoh saw his faithfulness to God, his integrity, righteousness, and knowledge. Daniel acknowledged God in all his ways, therefore, God honored him and gave him divine ability to serve the king without compromising his faith. God gave Daniel and his friends an unusual aptitude for understanding every aspect of literature and wisdom. God specifically gave Daniel the ability to interpret dreams.

Right then, I felt the love of God and wrote this prayer:

> *God, I thank You for speaking to me through Your word. I pray that You would give me an unusual aptitude for understanding every aspect of the Nevada Revised Statute, may you give me the ability to interpret the meaning of the law. Help me to operate in excellence, righteousness and integrity, and I thank You for favor with those in authority over me.*

There it was again, a "To Tressa, Love God" moment. I was reminded that no matter how much I thought someone else could not relate to what I was dealing with, God could absolutely relate to any and everything that I was going through. Through scripture, God spoke to me and me let me know that I was right where I needed to be, and that I was there because of His favor. Therefore, I did not need to be envious of anyone. He lovingly showed me what to pray specifically for my situation. My job was to let the light of Christ shine through me, be excellent, and do my work as though I was doing it for Him. God was acutely aware of my situation, and He was able to give me all the tools that I needed to be successful on my job without one bit of compromise.

Chapter
13

You're the One with Faith, Right?

Now faith is the substance of things hoped for;
the evidence of things not seen.
Hebrews 11:1 KJ

My phone rang, showing a 905 area code. Riverside. My heart started pounding in my chest. It was after ten at night. Taking a deep breath, I answered the phone.

"Hello?"

"Hello, is this this Tressa Fernandez?"

"Yes it is."

"*Mom, you have to come and get me right now*," came Jamar's voice from the background.

"Who is this?" I asked.

"Mrs. Fernandez this is Officer Stockton with the Riverside police. Do you know a Jamar Barker?"

Again, I heard from the background, *"Mom, help me please help me."*

"Yes, he is my son. Sir what's wrong?"

"I found your son on the side of the road, he is in distress, and he gave me this number to call," Officer Stockton said, "Ma'am where are you located?"

"I'm in Las Vegas."

"Are you able to get him a bus ticket to come home?"

"Sir, that's what I'm trying to do, but the next bus doesn't leave until tomorrow morning at nine."

I could still hear Jamar yelling in the background, begging me to come and get him. His voice was hoarse and raspy; he sounded so tired.

"Jamar, you need to calm down and be still," the officer said.

"Well Ma'am he can't stay here, I will take him to the bus station for him to wait there until his bus leaves."

"Thank you sir."

"Good-bye," he said.

I hung up the phone feeling sick, with my heart aching, Jamar had sounded so desperate. About an hour later the phone rang again, the same 905 area code.

"Hello?"

"Mrs. Fernandez, this is Officer Stockton again from the Riverside police. I've got Jamar here at the bus station; however, the bus station is closed."

"Mom, please help me, please don't let him leave me here, they will get me. I won't make it through the night, please don't let him leave me," Jamar screamed from the background.

"Jamar, calm down, you are going to be alright," said the officer.

"No! No! I won't, you can't leave me here! Mom, please don't let him leave me here."

"Ma'am. The bus station is closed, I am going to leave Jamar here on a bench in front of the bus station. What is his ticket confirmation number?"

"2334589JB" I replied.

"Ok, I've written it down on a piece of paper and given it to Jamar, so when the bus station opens in the morning, he will have his ticket information so he can get on the bus. I hope everything works out."

"Thank you."

"Mom, mom, please, I can't stay here, they will get me, I won't make it through the night," came Jamar's voice again from the background.

"Ok ma'am good-bye."

What was Jamar so afraid of? How was he going to make it through the night? There was no way he was going to just sit on a bench in front of the bus station all night! I pictured a lone bench under a streetlight on some deserted street, with Jamar there going crazy. I went into the bedroom where Al was in bed watching TV.

"Babe, Jamar is going through something out there in Riverside, the police have left him outside of the bus station, but it's closed, and the bus to Vegas doesn't leave until nine tomorrow morning. I am so worried; I don't know how he is going to make it through the night. It's about a three-hour drive to Riverside, can we drive down and get him?"

"No, we are not going to do that, I don't think it's a good idea. You're the one with the faith, right?" he said.

With tears welling up in my eyes, I stormed out of the room and went into my craft room. He was absolutely right. I was the one with the faith, and I knew what to do.

I picked up my phone, and did a group text to my PIC's (partners in Christ):

> *6/9/2017 10:31 pm*
> *PRAYER WARRIORS!*
>
> *I need your prayers right now! Jamar is on drugs. The Riverside police have just dropped him off in front of the bus station, which is closed. He has a ticket to get back to Vegas that doesn't leave until 9:00 a.m. tomorrow. Please pray that he would be safe, stay at the bus station and get on that bus tomorrow. Thank you! This is not too hard for God, please link your faith with mine that he will make it through the night and get back to Vegas safely.*

I got down on my knees, and I prayed and prayed. I cried out to God and prayed for my son's deliverance, for his safety, protection and that he would make it through the night and get on that bus. I prayed for the Holy Spirit to move, for God to save him and get him home. Then I got up, wiped my tears and went to bed and fell asleep praying.

When I got up the next morning, I continued to pray and began to prepare for Intercessory Prayer at church which I was leading that day. I asked for God's divine enablement to help me to be able to lead prayer. Prayer started at 9:00 a.m., the time that the bus was scheduled to leave Riverside. As I mounted the pulpit, I did not know if Jamar was on the bus. As I led prayer, I asked those that were at prayer to pray with me for Jamar. At about 11:30 a.m. my phone rang, an area code I didn't know.

"Hello?"

"Mom?"

"Jamar?"

"Mom, I'm on the bus."

I sagged with relief and began to praise God. By the power of the Holy Ghost and God's divine intervention, He had protected my son through the night, he got on that bus with no identification, only the ticket confirmation number and was on his way home.

Once again, God had spoken. This time, He'd used my husband, who does not know Him (yet) to remind me that the answer wasn't to jump in my car and drive to Riverside, to take matters into my own hands and go running to my son's rescue. The answer was to pray, have faith, and trust God to move. The answer was to cast my cares upon Him because He cared about me. The answer was for me to understand that God would perfect that which concerned me.

God saved my son's life that night. He brought him out of darkness into the light, life and light of Christ; and I am eternally grateful. There was still a long road ahead, but at least Jamar was still alive with a chance to travel that road with God with him every step of the way.

CHAPTER

14

A PAGA MOMENT

Call to me and I will answer you and tell
you great and unsearchable things you do not know.
Jeremiah 33:3 NIV

ON THIS PARTICULAR DAY I STARTED MY BIBLE
study time with a prayer that went something like this:

"Lord, as I read Your word today, I pray that You would
give to me a spirit of wisdom and revelation in the knowledge
of You. I know that entrance into Your word gives light and
understanding to the simple. I ask for understanding today, I
pray that You would show me in the scriptures something that
I have not seen before, speak to my heart Lord. Amen."

I checked my Bible reading plan to see where to begin
for the day, then opened my Bible to John chapter 4. As I
read, I came to John 4:34 CSB: "My food is to do the will
of Him who sent me and to finish His work." Jesus told

them." My food? I stopped to consider this. I thought about what food does to the physical body; it builds you up, gives you strength, makes you grow. After eating, you are satisfied, fulfilled. A few questions bubbled up in mind: Jesus got nourishment, satisfaction and fulfillment from doing what God told Him to do? He was filled up, satisfied, no longer hungry by being obedient? Obedience caused Him to grow? I had never thought of obedience in this way.

I went to one of my favorite Bible commentaries, the Life Application Study Bible and found this note on v 34: *The "nourishment" about which Jesus was speaking was his spiritual nourishment. It includes more than Bible study, prayer, and attending church. Spiritual nourishment also comes from doing God's will and helping to bring his work of salvation to completion. We are nourished not only by what we take in, but also by what we give out for God. In John 17:4, Jesus refers to completing God's work on earth.* The note referred me to Matthew 4:4:

But Jesus told him, "No! The Scriptures say, 'People do not live by bread alone, but by every word that comes from the mouth of God.'"

I went back to the Bible. John 4:35-39 (Jesus speaking) it read, "Don't you say, 'There are still four more months, then comes the harvest? Listen to what I'm telling you: Open your eyes and look at the fields, for they are ready for harvest. The reaper is already receiving pay and gathering fruit for eternal life, so the sower and reaper can rejoice together. For in this case the saying is true: 'One sows, and another reaps.' I sent you to reap what you didn't labor for; others have labored, and you have benefited from their labor. Now many Samaritans from that town believed in Him because of what the woman said when she testified, "He told me everything I ever did."

The words leapt off the page. I must be a witness! The harvest is ripe! The power of my testimony. Do I believe? These words were spoken by Jesus Himself, if I believe them as I say I do, then I must step out in faith and witness! I must plant seeds. Any person that does not receive the Lord when I witness or the Soul Winning Action Team (S.W.A.T.) goes out, a seed is planted that someone else can harvest. We should rejoice, seed planted! Often times when the S.W.A.T. team goes out, not one person that we minister to receives the Lord as their Savior, which is a bit discouraging at times. However, God spoke to me through these scriptures and answered my prayer. In the past when I had read these scriptures, I had never noticed that Jesus was nourished by doing what God instructed Him to do, He was enriched by planting and sowing seeds. Sometimes in witnessing we will be the seed planter, sometimes we will be the reaper. Just because someone doesn't answer the call to salvation when I minister to them doesn't mean that God isn't moving.

I have said so many times that souls are the most important thing to God, yet, I do not witness! I say I want to live a life that is pleasing to God, and the thing that pleases Him most is people getting saved! Therefore, I must go about my day thinking about how I can plant seeds!

Since the COVID-19 pandemic began in March of 2020 the S.W.A.T. team has not been able to go out witnessing. Recently our Pastor challenged our leadership staff and asked us what we were doing since we could not come to church and asked if we had witnessed to anyone. Now that God had me thinking about being nourished by doing what He (through my Pastor) had asked me to do, I thought, *"How can we witness during the pandemic?"* I had barely finished the thought when God responded, *through the mail.* A plan unfolded that could only have been from the Lord. The thoughts were coming so quickly that my fingers could not type fast enough!

I knew I needed to share my testimony; the Samaritan woman went and told people about her encounter with the Lord and they were saved! I prayed:

> *Lord, I thank You and praise You and acknowledge You in the writing of this letter. I ask that You guide my footsteps and direct my path in what to write and what to say, so that Your will would be done in reaping the harvest of souls to the Kingdom. Help me to be a witness for You, I want to get nourishment from being obedient to You, by planting seeds, by reaping the harvest in Jesus name!*

With God's divine enablement, I wrote a short note with my testimony. Something that could be slipped into a thank-you card and left with a waiter at a restaurant, the cashier at the store, whoever God prompted me to. Seeds planted!

I have been praying regularly for my cousin's salvation. I had made few feeble attempts to reach out to him but had not connected. I wrote him a letter that day and dropped it in the mail, praying all the way. Seed planted.

I had just had a paga moment with God. An encounter that changed my whole perspective on witnessing. God spoke to me and answered my prayer to open my eyes so I could see the hope of His calling in a way that He never had before. Prior to this, when God spoke it was regarding something specific to me or a personal situation I was dealing with. This time it was so much bigger than me. Lives are at stake, help me Lord, to move past hearing and totally and completely do what You have asked me to do.

CHAPTER
15

SOME OTHER TESTIMONIES

*And they have defeated him by the blood of
the Lamb and by their testimony.*
Revelation 12:11 NLT

BY NOW, I THINK YOU'RE GETTING THE GIST
of it. God has spoken to me in many different ways
throughout my life, and these are just a few examples. Some
things you keep to yourself, wink, wink. However, God also
speaks to other people, shocking I know. That's the thing
that is so awesome about God; He is no respecter of per-
sons. He has equal and unconditional love for every single
one of us; He does not play favorites. When we listen for
His voice, He shows us His perfect plan and destiny for
our lives. I have heard many testimonies from family and
friends of the ways in which God has spoken to them and
want to share a few of them with you. Just so you know

that it's not only me (although I like to believe I'm God's favorite). The testimonies on the following pages are from three of my friends that God divinely connected me with so their stories could be in this book.

Saving Grayce: I met Grayce James at church about three years ago, and we connected right away. She was in the middle of getting her PhD. She has since completed it and is now Dr. Grayce James. We don't talk often but when we do, it is always a God connection. We think the phone call is for a casual conversation to catch up, and it almost always ends up where one of us is lifting the other up and with a word of encouragement specific to the situation the other is currently experiencing.

Visions and Dreams: Josephine Thomas, Mrs. J as I call her, has always been a woman of great wisdom to me. As the head of the hospitality team at church, she is graced with the ability to lead a team of people in a very no-nonsense way, always seeking the Lord first and speaking the truth in love. Her unwavering prayer covering for her husband and children encourages me to continually do the same for mine. When she was diagnosed with cancer and underwent surgery, chemo and all of the side effects that go with it, she handled it with strength and grace. She sought the Lord, received counseling from our Pastors, remained steadfast in prayer, spoke the word only and emerged on the other side of it cancer-free and praising God.

Grace, Love and Mercy: The connection that I made with my friend through our jobs was immediate. We always worked well together and did whatever we could to support each other. Somewhere along the way, I learned that she was a Christian and our friendship was further solidified. When she shared her story with me, I was moved to tears and knew I wanted to share it in the pages of this book. She has asked to remain anonymous but desires to share her story hoping that it will bring restoration of hope and healing to others and bring glory to God.

I pray that you will be blessed by their testimonies. I am honored that they would share their stories with me. I thank God that He has used me to share their stories with you.

CHAPTER

16

SAVING GRAYCE

For He will order His angels to protect
you wherever you go.
Psalm 91:11 NLT

WHEN I WOKE UP ON NOVEMBER 11, 2019, I was prompted to pray Psalm 91 over myself. This was unusual, because typically I would pray the prayer for family, friends and others that God put on my heart. I got ready for work and the feeling continued on the drive to work. I could not shake it, and as I was getting out of the car, I felt really pressed to pray Psalm 91. I felt that if I did not pray right then and there, there would be a problem; I did not feel secure getting out of the car without praying Psalm 91 over myself.

Lord, I thank You that You are my refuge and fortress, I trust You with this day today, and thank You for covering me with Your feathers, I take refuge under the protection of Your wings, I will not be afraid of what the day brings, whatever happens, I will only see it with my eyes, it will not come near me. You are my dwelling place, so no evil or bad thing will come near me. I thank You for Your angels all around me protecting me and keeping me. Thank You for delivering me, thank You for being with me in trouble, thank You for long life, in Jesus name, amen.

I went into work with a peace regarding a situation that had been brewing at work. I am a teacher at a women's correctional institution and had been preparing a class to take their GED exam. The week prior, I had let an inmate off the hook for throwing coffee in class. When the guard asked me what I wanted to do, I decided to allow the woman to stay in class. What she had done was small to me, but a major infraction that normally would have resulted in her being removed from class and put in solitary confinement for at least six months. I didn't believe that throwing coffee warranted her missing out on the opportunity to get her GED.

There had been some recent situations where inmates had brought items into the classroom that were not allowed, and it was causing problems. As a result, when the incident occurred in my classroom, others on my job were angry and felt the woman should have been punished and not allowed to stay in class. I believed that the need to pray Psalm 91 was for my protection regarding the drama at work.

My boss called a meeting that day with all of the staff, I was not surprised and was prepared to receive pushback because of how I had handled the situation in my classroom. However, during the meeting the situation was addressed in a general way and everyone was reminded about the importance of following the rules when an inmate commits an infraction, and that was the end of it. I was grateful and thanked God for His protection through Psalm 91 and I didn't think anything else about it as I went about the rest of my day.

On the drive home that evening I was sitting at an intersection that was a four-way stop. I let the person on my left go ahead of me, and then I started through the intersection when WHAM! I was hit on the passenger side. I spun out of control; I had no sense of direction or what was going on, my heart was pounding in my chest, and I was shaking. The car kept spinning, trees were scraping the doors, the car was bouncing around, and I was holding my breath.

Press on the brakes.

I pressed on the brakes and when I looked up, I saw nothing but a gray cinderblock wall. The smelled of burned rubber was in the air. I put the car in park, got out and ran, not knowing if the car was about to explode.

People started coming from what seemed like everywhere asking me if I was ok. "Are you alright, you took out that whole curb and three trees!" said one guy who had witnessed the whole thing. The man who had hit me also came and checked on me. There were so many people checking on me, and so much compassion from everyone I encountered.

I called my co-worker and she called our boss, who lived not far from where the accident occurred, and she came right away. I could not stop shaking, and while I was giving a statement to the police, my boss went about taking pictures, and helping in any way she could until my son arrived. When we went to look at my car, it was then that I realized that it was God that had told me to put on the brakes. My car had stopped mere inches from the cinder-block wall. "Grayce, you are a blessed woman," my boss said as we looked at what could have been. Prior to hearing "press on the brakes" it had not occurred to me to put on the brakes. I had absolutely no sense of what was happening until I heard the voice of God.

Sometimes we think God is speaking about one thing, when actually His divine purpose and plan is for something else beyond our knowledge. I had started off the day with a thank You Jesus after the meeting at work, but after the accident, it was a hallelujah to God for saving me from crashing through a wall. I walked away from that accident without a scratch, and my boss, who does not yet know the Lord, was able to witness the hand of the Lord upon my life. I had a divine intervention that day, that started with me listening when God spoke to me to pray Psalm 91.

Chapter

17

Visions and Dreams

For God may speak in one way, or in another
yet man does not perceive it.
In a dream, in a vision of the night,
when deep sleep falls upon men,
while slumbering in their beds,
then He opens the ears of men,
and seals their instruction.
Job 33:14-16 NKJ

GOD HAS SPOKEN TO ME FROM AN EARLY AGE, one of my clearest memories is from early in my marriage. I was a "homebody": I enjoyed staying at home and being with my family. My husband, however, enjoyed going out, partying and hanging with the fellas. He would come home late at night, long after I had gone to bed. Over time, I convinced myself that he was having an affair. I didn't have any proof, just call it women's intuition. Not knowing God very well at the time, I just went with that.

I woke up one morning and made up my mind; I was going to get a divorce. God said no. Since my mind was made up, I knew it couldn't be God, so I said, "Devil, you are a liar, I'm getting a divorce I don't have to live like this." I knew of a divorce lawyer downtown that did not require payment up front. I was almost at the lawyer's office, and I can't tell you what happened. I don't know if I blacked out or passed out or what, but when I came to my senses, my car was turned around, and I was heading in the opposite direction of the attorney's office. I hadn't hit anything or anyone, but people were looking, and the car was headed back home. God said, *"I didn't say you could do this."* I was so shaken, what had happened? How did it happen? I had no idea; but I pulled myself together and headed home. I cried all the way, having a conversation with God because I did not feel that He was being fair to me. The Bible said if he commits adultery I could leave, but if You're telling me to stay, I don't think the Bible is real. I got home and went in the house. God said, *"The Bible is real; I didn't tell you to get a divorce."* That's all God said to me. I never said anything else after that. I never thought of divorce again; the incident on the way to the divorce lawyer scared the life out of me. I still do not know how my car got turned around.

It was eight years later before I knew why God said I could not get a divorce. My husband's mother passed, and prior to that, I never thought about praying for my husband because my mother-in-law always took care of that and frankly, I was a bit jealous, so I didn't pray. After she passed, as clear as day God spoke to me and said, *"Now you need to pray for him."* That is when I started praying for my husband until God saved him. He is now saved, filled with the Holy Ghost, loves the Lord, reads the word, and prays all the time. If I had divorced him, he may have never gotten saved. I learned then that the key to listening to God is not having your mind made up about what you want the answer to be. All those years ago, it didn't matter if my husband was being faithful or not. God had a plan for his life, I was a part of the plan, and my husband's soul was at stake.

Every mother knows if their son is saved or not. My son had people fooled, he knew how to dress, what to say and how to act. He knew to say yes ma'am, and no sir. He knew church; he had been raised in church. He went to church because he was made to go. My rule was if you live in my house, you're going to church. I was watching his life, and I knew he wasn't saved. When he turned eighteen, I called him into the kitchen and said to him "John Jr., choose this day who you will serve, don't play church, God is nothing to play with." He said yes ma'am and left the house. Two weeks later I had a dream, and there was a tornado. Not like a widespread tornado that you see on TV; it was narrow and headed directly to my house. I was returning home and I could see the tornado. I thought to myself, *"I'm not going to make it home."* I held on to a fence near my house and when I looked up into the tornado, I could see the sunlight, but the rain and wind were heavy, however, the storm passed me over. I made it home and opened the door, someone else was already in the house, but I didn't see their face. I said, "Let me help you out of those wet clothes." My daughter said, "Mom, that storm is headed for California were John Jr. is." I said, "By the time it gets there, it will have dissipated."

The dream was very clear. I knew this was God. I woke my husband up. "Sweetie, we need to pray. Something is going to happen, and it's going to be bad, and it's going to be just us."

Two weeks later John Jr. came home from work, grabbed his backpack and headed out the door. As he left, something came over me, and I immediately began to pray. John and I were in the bed, about 8:00 p.m. when there was a knock on the door. It was the police, wanting to know who owned a red car. John told them he owned a red car, but John Jr. was driving it. They explained that there had been a shooting and the car had been shot up. I excused myself from the room and sent John Jr. a text and told him that he needed to come home and he needed to tell the truth to the police. When he got home, he sat on the sofa and talked to the police, calm as calm can be, but my husband and I knew he was lying. We knew that the police knew he was lying. The police allowed us to talk to John Jr. alone before they took him to the detectives' office to talk to ask him more questions. When we talked to John Jr., we told him we knew he was lying and that the police knew he was lying.

We later received a call from UMC Trauma center saying that John Jr. was okay and was going to be charged with discharging a firearm in public and he could be bailed out. We were confused by this, and didn't understand why UMC was calling, had the police hurt him? What was going on? John Jr. called at about 3:00 a.m. for us to pick him up. When he got home and went to get in the bathroom to get in the shower, and I could hear what sounded like pellets dropping on the floor. I said, "John Jr., what happened?" He said, "I was shot."

"Let me see," I said.

When he pulled off his shirt and I saw his back, I could not breathe. I thought that if he had been any closer to the shooter, a hole the size of Texas would have been blown in his back and he would be dead. When I caught my breath I said, "Lord, I thank You." Then he told me some of what had happened. God brought the dream back to me, by the time the person that shot John Jr. got their shotgun, he was far enough away that when he got shot, the bullets dissipated. In the dream this was the storm that had dissipated by the time it got to him. The person that I had seen in the house was John Jr.

Two weeks later, I had another dream, and there was another storm, with all my family members except John Jr. I knew at that point John Jr. was going to prison. God continued to speak to me through the ordeal. Initially, when he was being sentenced, God had softened the judge's heart, and he was going to be issued a lighter sentence and be released home on house arrest. Two days before the sentencing, God spoke to me and said, "If I let him come home now, he will do worse." Before we went to court, I already knew John Jr. would not be coming home, however God had not released me to share that with my husband and family. When the judge sentenced John Jr. to serve time, I was not moved, because I already knew. My husband was upset, and my other children were crying. When we got in the car to head home, I told my daughter, "Please stop crying, John Jr. is going to come home, he's just not coming home right now." She asked, "How do you know?" and I told her what God had told me. I told my daughter that I would rather see him in jail, than do something and end up dead. When John Jr. was sentenced to prison the Holy Ghost asked me, *"What are you going to do now?"* I said, "I'm going to cry and I'm going to pray until You send John Jr. home." I was never worried about him while he was in prison because God had already spoken to me that he was going to bring him home safely.

During this time, I had to have an open mind and listen for God. I had to stay in the word to know if it was God or the devil speaking to me. I stood on the word of God because through the ordeal with my son, God spoke to me through what my Pastors taught me; to not be moved by what I saw, felt, or heard, but only be moved by the word of God. If it had not been for that word and other words spoken to me by my Pastors, I would not have made it. I would have had sleepless nights. Through the seven-year ordeal I only had one sleepless night. I thank God for speaking to me, and that over years I have learned to listen.

CHAPTER
18

LOVE, GRACE, AND MERCY

And He said to me, "My grace is sufficient for you,
for my strength is made perfect in weakness."
2 Corinthians 12:9 NKJ

MY HUSBAND HAD BEEN WORKING OUT OF town on a large construction project and very unexpectedly passed in his sleep. I was in complete shock and pain when I got the call early on a Thursday morning. Many family, friends, and co-workers immediately came to share their sympathies, surrounding me with their love, prayers, and support. At first, I was in a state of shock; then, very busy with much to handle with the various responsibilities of funeral arrangements, business things to handle, and questions to answer. People came over with meals, sharing their sympathies, feelings of loss, regrets, stories, and memories. Then it came after several weeks; my body was finally beyond exhaustion. I had fallen asleep for a couple of hours, and as I was waking up, I realized that for the first time since getting the call, that day I was completely alone. Everyone had gone back home, there was no longer anyone staying with me, there were no appointments to deal with, no one would be stopping by. That day I faced the passing and loss of my husband without a single other distraction. The pain of this realization was so intense and heavy; it had its own gravity that left not an ounce of strength within me.

As I was in bed crying, I prayed for God to help me find the strength to simply get out of bed. After a while, I was able to get out of bed, only to make it around the corner to my closet and collapse to the floor, sobbing with pain, crying and speaking of my pain and loss to God; I began quoting Isaiah 41:10 and other verses of comfort of God's promises and love. I was on my knees, humbled, broken in spirit and soul, quoting scriptures between sobs and tears. After some time of this, I went from sobbing from the pain, to crying out, "Why God? How could You do this to me! How could you take my partner in life so soon and unexpectedly?" Right in the middle of my tirade, I heard a calm voice in my spirit very clearly; so audible that I stopped in the middle of what I was venting and heard:

Lean not on your own understanding, for My ways are not your ways.

I remained in silence, and the next thing my heart and mind saw was a vision of what I think it must have been like for Moses pushing his face into a crevice of the rock so that

God's glory could pass by him. The afterglow of God's glory just passing by Moses was so intense that Moses had to wear a veil over his face as not to scare the people of Israel, and he didn't even look at God; this was just from the mere passing of God's glory! I heard in my spirit that we are so simple, so unable and lacking in our ability. God doesn't show us all of His ways because we don't even begin to have the ability to understand His ways.

If I had told you and you knew you would only get to have him for a certain time; would you still have wanted the time and memories with him?

I looked up and said, "Yes, Lord, of course! I would want every minute of it again! He was a great man and partner that I loved and respected very much."

Then why are you choosing to be angry with Me instead of giving Me praise and thanks for the time that you had?

I heard the word "choosing" specifically enunciated; as to make my spirit aware of the fact that at that moment, I was choosing to go down a path of anger and bitterness instead of praising and thanking God for the blessing of love, memories and time that I had. I realized that I was in control of what I chose to focus on. I then began to ask God for forgiveness; I repented for yelling at God, for questioning Him; me so pitiful, weak, knowing nothing.

I began to thank and praise Him, for giving me a man that I loved and respected, for blessing me with the opportunity to experience love, to have such wonderful memories. I thanked Him for blessing me with such an outpouring of love and support by family, friends, and co-workers. As I was praising Him, I realized how emotionally drained I was, how much energy such anger takes. I praised Him even more for loving me so much that He stopped me so quickly from going down such a wasted path of anger, that He heard my cry and poured out his grace, mercy, and love so quickly.

It is still hard; I love and miss my husband tremendously, but praise be to God that His promises are true! Praise Him that I do not have to run from or hide from the pain, for it is truly greater than I can bear. But I can run to Him for healing and restoration of my heart and soul; I can praise and thank Him for such love, such comfort, and it is amazing how His love, grace, and mercy continually pour into me and restore my soul.

CHAPTER

19

GOD IS SPEAKING

That is why the Holy Spirit says,
"Today when you hear his voice,
don't harden your hearts as Israel did when
they rebelled,
when they tested me in the wilderness."
Hebrews 3:7-8 NLT

GOD SPEAKS TO US, AND THE BIBLE IS REPLETE with accounts of God speaking in many different ways. It is important for us to know how God speaks. The testimonies I've shared demonstrate how God speaks, and I would be remiss if I didn't back the stories up with Biblical accounts of the ways that God speaks.

An example of God speaking through circumstances is found in the book of Jonah. Initially, God spoke directly to Jonah, but he did not listen. Then God spoke to Jonah through circumstances, first when He was swallowed by a whale, then a vine grew to provide shade to Jonah, and it withered. Jonah tried to ignore God, but God would not have it and resorted to other ways to get his attention. Take a look at your circumstances, and ask yourself, *what is God speaking to me through these circumstances?*

As we know, God can speak through people. There are several examples of this in the Bible, but one that stands out to me is when the prophet Nathan came to David and told him a story about two men, one rich and one poor, and the rich man took the poor man's sheep. David's quick and angry response was that the man deserved to die. Nathan the prophet told David that he was that man because he had stolen Uriah's wife, Bathsheba, and had Uriah killed. God spoke to David through Nathan and used him to show David the error of what he had done (2 Samuel chapters 11 and 12). God has spoken to me many times through my Pastors to show me where I needed to make changes. I thank God for the opportunity to make mid-term corrections!

God also speaks through visions and dreams. This is shown in the lives of Joseph, Solomon, Jacob, Peter, Paul and many others. The most epic (in my opinion) was God speaking to John in the book of Revelations. John received a vision from Christ, and he recorded it for the churches in Asia, but also for us as Christians. Another of my favorites is in Acts 9 when God spoke to Ananias in a dream and told him to go and lay hands on Saul so he could receive his sight. At first Ananias questioned God, after all, Saul had been persecuting Christians! God told Ananias that Saul was His chosen one to witness to the Gentiles. After God spoke, Ananias went and did what God told him to do. Saul received his sight back and went on to become Paul, one of the greatest apostles ever that wrote over two-thirds of the New Testament. Imagine if Ananias had not done what God told him to do. The implications are unfathomable.

The Bible promises blessings to those who listen to its words and do what it says. Of the eighteen times that the phrase "He that has ears to hear, let him hear" is used in the New Testament (New King James Bible), eight of them are in the book of Revelations! That is worth taking heed to and ensuring that we are listening for and hearing God's voice, then doing what He's calling us to do.

Then there's God speaking through supernatural manifestations. He spoke to Moses through a burning bush (Exodus 3:1). He spoke to Saul on the Damascus road through a bright light (Acts 9:1). He got Saul's attention in such a way that his life was changed forever!

He spoke to Elijah through a still small voice in 1 Kings 19:12. Nowadays, with so much going on, we must take time to be still before God so we can hear Him. Before I came to know God, I was so busy sinning, I could not hear Him. Like the Israelites in Jeremiah 7:13, while I was sinning, God was trying to talk to me, but I wouldn't listen. I'm so grateful that I finally stood still, and listened, hallelujah!

And of course, God speaks to us through His word, the Bible. The scripture itself is the voice of God. It is alive and active (Hebrews 4:12), a mirror to show us ourselves and show us how to live a life that is pleasing to God.

I pray that it is clearer than ever before that God is speaking to YOU. In the simple things, it could be a simple prompting to call or text someone you haven't spoken to in a while. Don't brush that thought off. My sister recently shared with me how she was prompted to call someone who had reached out to her. Her initial response was to text them, which she did. However, the thought to call didn't go away. She called thinking it would be a conversation about one thing, but it ended up being an opportunity to minister to the person and really encourage them with prayer and scripture.

I began writing down these testimonies in 2013, and even as I have gathered them together for this book, I can see how I have grown, and continue to grow. There have been times when I was so consumed with life happening although I would pray, I wouldn't take time to hear God. But I'm getting better. I hope that you will learn His voice as you continue in your journey with the Lord. Listen for Him. He is always speaking. He is our loving, caring, sharing, heavenly Father, and He is deeply concerned with every detail of our lives. I pray that you would evolve from hearing, to listening and ultimately doing the word that you hear. Your life will be better because of it.

God is speaking, are you listening?

CHAPTER

20

THE BEST GIFT

For by grace you have been saved through faith,
and not that of yourselves; it is the gift of God,
Ephesians 2:8 NKJ

I HOPE THAT YOU ALREADY HAVE A RELATION-
ship with God and have accepted Him as your Lord and
Savior. If not, I pray that as you have read these pages, God
has spoken to your heart, and you are ready to receive the
best gift ever. If you believe in your heart that Jesus Christ
lived, died and rose again, then pray the following prayer:

Lord Jesus, I need You. Thank You for dying on
the cross for my sins. I open the door of my life
and receive You as my Savior and Lord. Thank
You for forgiving my sins and giving me eternal

life. Take control of my life. Make me the kind of person You want me to be.

How do you know you are saved? Trust and believe God and His word to be true! Now that you have received Jesus as your Lord and Savior, a few things have happened:

- *Christ came into your life. (Revelation 3:20; Colossians 1:27)*
- *Your sins were forgiven. (Colossians 1:14)*
- *You became a child of God. (John 1:12)*
- *You received eternal life. (John 5:24)*
- *You began the great adventure for which God created you. (John 10:10; 2 Corinthians 5:17; 1 Thessalonians 5:18)*

This is just the beginning!

A few things to help you to grow in the new life:

1. Get a Bible and read it every day, John is a great place to start.
2. Pray daily.
3. Connect with a church, Destiny Christian Center is a great place to connect with God and other believers and develop your relationship with Him! Find out more at www.dcclv.org.

God is Speaking,
Are You Listening?

Journal Prompts

"Thus says the Lord, the God of Israel:
Write in a book all the words that I have
spoken to you"
Jeremiah 30:2 ESV

NOW IT'S YOUR TURN. DUST OFF THAT
journal that you got for a Christmas gift last year and didn't
know what to write in it. You can also write in the space provided after each prompt. The following prompts are created
to help you to think back on your life and identify times
when God has spoken to you. Write them down so you
can see your journey and your growth in the Lord. This
can be your personal journal to refer to at times in your life
when you're wondering where God is. You will be able to
look back at your own experiences, your own testimonies,
and see that God has been right there with you all along,

speaking to you, guiding you, and continually calling you to come closer to Him.

When you're writing take time to try and remember all the details, and answer these questions as you respond to each of the journal prompts:

- When did it happen?
- Who were the people involved?
- What scriptures were used?
- How did you feel?
- Did you make a change right then, or later, or at all?
- When did you realize that it was God speaking?

As you write, don't think about grammar, how it sounds, or if it's "right". Let the thoughts flow freely from your memory. Don't be critical about what you write, this is about getting your memories down on paper. Once you've got it all down you can go back and refine it if you'd like. I don't recommend trying to answer all of the journal prompts at one time. Don't rush the process, ask God to help you remember. For me the process took many years, many of the memories I had conveniently tucked deep in the recesses of my mind. The prompts provided are a few suggestions to get you going. I hope that as you complete them you will continue creating your own collection of testimonies. Enjoy the journey.

Have you ever been in a church service and the minister spoke something that was specific to your situation, in a way that made it feel like there was no one else in the room?

_____

_____

_____

_____

_____

_____

_____

_____

_____

_____

_____

_____

_____

Prior to knowing God, have you had any experiences where you should have been seriously injured, arrested, or even died but the situation turned out in your favor in an inexplicable way?

_____

_____

_____

_____

_____

_____

_____

_____

_____

_____

_____

_____

_____

Have you ever had a paga moment like I did in Chapter 14? Describe a time when you read a familiar scripture, maybe one you've read many times before, or one you've read for the first time. But on a particular instance you saw something you had never seen before, or you understood it in a way you never had before.

_____

_____

_____

_____

_____

_____

_____

_____

_____

_____

_____

_____

_____

_____

Is there a time that one person or encounter turned your life completely around, like my experience with the BJC factor?

_____

_____

_____

_____

_____

_____

_____

_____

_____

_____

_____

_____

_____

_____

Has God spoken to you through a vision or dream, like in Mrs. Josephine's story?

_____

_____

_____

_____

_____

_____

_____

_____

_____

_____

_____

_____

_____

_____

Have you ever been in the middle of a crisis in your life perhaps crying and hysterical, or angry and yelling, then heard a voice and suddenly felt great peace, similar to the experience of the Anonymous Child of God?

_____

_____

_____

_____

_____

_____

_____

_____

_____

_____

_____

_____

_____

Have you ever had a dream that was so vivid and real, then the events in the dream happened in real-life, something like in Mrs. Josephine's Story?

_____

_____

_____

_____

_____

_____

_____

_____

_____

_____

_____

_____

_____

_____

REFERENCES

Power of a Praying Wife, Stormie O'Martian

8 Steps to Living Peaceably With Your Unsaved Husband taken from *Pull Up A Chair Blog* October 2006, Kate Plourde

---

Visit Tressa's website at: www.tressafernandez.com

Share your testimony with Tressa at godisspeaking@gmail.com

9 781662 805202